by Michelle Kerner
Illustrated by Ron Lipking

Glenview, Illinois • Boston, Massachusetts • Mesa, Arizona
Shoreview, Minnesota • Upper Saddle River, New Jersey

Dog ran into the barn. "I have **BIG** news!" he barked.

"Big news?" asked Donkey.

"What is it, Dog?" asked Cow. "What is this all about?"

"We are going to have a new baby!" Dog said.

"A new baby?" clucked the hens.

"Yes," Dog barked. "A baby pig, a piglet! I saw him already. He is only two weeks old!"

Cow looked at all the animals. "Do you know what this means?" she asked.

"What does it mean?" asked Dog. The animals looked scared.

"It means we must clean the barn!" said Cow.

The animals nodded. "We shall clean!" they agreed.

They started to work. They picked things up. They put things down. Soon they were tired, but the barn was still messy!

"Look at this mess!" said Cow. "We need to work together!"

"The work will go faster if we sing," said Rooster.

The animals started to sing:

Let's work together,
It's easier that way!
Let's work together,
Piglet is coming today!

Each animal took a job. Donkey carried sticks outside. Dog stacked the sticks. Cat piled bags of seeds. The hens picked up the corn.

Cow found some hay. "For Piglet's bed," she said.

Rooster had a job too. He watched for Piglet.

"The barn is nice and clean!" said Cow proudly. "We did a good job working together!"

Then Rooster crowed the **BIG** news. "Piglet is here!"